The Don't Laugh Challenge™

9 YEAR OLD EDITION

Don't Laugh Challenge
BONUS PLAY

Join our Joke Club and get the Bonus Play PDF!

Simply send us an email to:

bacchuspublish@gmail.com

and you will get the following:

• **10 BONUS** hilarious jokes!

• An entry in our Monthly Giveaway of a $25 Amazon Gift card!

We draw a new winner each month and will contact you via email!

Good luck!

Welcome to
The Don't Laugh Challenge ™

• How do you play?

The Don't Laugh Challenge is made up of 10 rounds with 2 games in each round. It is a 2-3 player game with the players being 'Jester #1', 'Jester #2', and a 'King' or 'Queen'. In each game you have an opportunity to score points by making the other players laugh.

After completing each round, tally up the points to determine the Round Champion! Add all 10 rounds together to see who is the Ultimate Don't Laugh Challenge Master! If you end up in a tie, use our final Tie Breaker Round for a Winner Takes All!

• Who can play the game?

Get the whole family involved! Grab a family member or a friend and take turns going back and forth. We've also added Bonus Points in game 2, so grab a 3rd person, a.k.a 'King' or 'Queen', and earn an extra point by making them guess your scene!

The Don't Laugh Challenge™ Activity Rules

- ## Game 1 - Jokes (1 point each)

  Jester #1 will hold the book and read each joke to Jester #2. If the joke makes Jester #2 laugh, Jester #1 can record a point for the joke. Each joke is worth 1 point. At the end of the jokes, tally up your total Joke Points scored for Jester #1 and continue to Game 2!

- ## Game 2 - Silly Scenarios (2 points each + bonus point)

  Without telling the other Jester what the scenarios say, read each scenario to yourself and then get creative by acting it out! You can use sound effects, but be sure not to say any words! If you make the other Jester laugh, record your points and continue to the next scenario.

  BONUS POINT: Get your parents or a third player, a.k.a King or Queen, involved and have them guess what in the world you are doing! Get the King or Queen to guess the scene correctly and you score a BONUS POINT!

The Don't Laugh Challenge ™
Activity Rules

Once Jester #1 completes both games it is Jester #2's turn. The directions at the bottom of the book will tell you who goes next. Once you have both completed all the games in the round, add your total points from each game to the Round Score Page and record the Round winner!

● How do you get started?

Flip a coin. If guessed correctly, then that Jester begins!

Tip: Make any of the activities extra funny by using facial expressions, funny voices or silly movements!

ROUND 1

Jokes

How did the box of crayons do on the pilot exam?
It passed with flying colors!

/1

What do you call a female creature that is half-horse, half-fish?
A MARE-maid!

/1

What do you call a self-centered dinosaur?
A Me-Rex.

/1

How do you make glass panes for a gingerbread house?
With win-DOUGH.

/1

JOKES TOTAL: _____ /4

Silly Scenarios

(Act it out!)

You're caught in a rainstorm. Every time a drop of rain hits you, you begin to melt little by little. Try and get inside before you're a puddle!

_____ /2

You are a jester in the King's Court. He orders you to juggle apples, but you don't know how. Try your best not to disappoint the King!

_____ /2

SILLY SCENARIOS TOTAL: _____ /4

NOW, PASS THE BOOK TO JESTER 2 ➡️

Jokes

JESTER 2

What do you call it when a chair falls over?
A bad SIT-uation!

/1

What do cards do for fun?
Go Fish!

/1

What do you call a tired jungle cat?
A PANT-ther.

/1

Why did the UFO'S break-up?
They needed space!

/1

JOKES TOTAL: ____ /4

Silly Scenarios

(Act it out!)

You're late to the rodeo and there's no time to get ready. Hope the judges are impressed when you do your makeup and hair... while riding a bucking bronco!

_____ /2

Pretend you're a cockroach crawling around when suddenly, a human scares you! Fall on your back and try to turn over with all your might!

_____ /2

SILLY SCENARIOS TOTAL: _____ /4

TIME TO SCORE YOUR POINTS! ➜

JESTER 1

/8
_____
ROUND TOTAL

JESTER 2

/8
_____
ROUND TOTAL

_____

ROUND
CHAMPION

ROUND 2

Jokes

What kind of dance do sinks do?

TAP Dance!   /1

What do you call it when you mix vegetables and music together?

Two peas in an iPod!   /1

What do you call bread that gets injured in a fight?

Toast!   /1

Where do Alaskans keep their money?

At the snow bank.   /1

JOKES TOTAL: _____ /4

Silly Scenarios

(Act it out!)

You need to tell your family that your train is leaving in 30 minutes, but you can only communicate using interpretive dance! HURRY!

/2

Cast out your fishing line and reel in the biggest fish on this side of the Atlantic! Pretend the fish is putting up a big fight, so be strong and don't fall in!

/2

SILLY SCENARIOS TOTAL: _____ /4

NOW, PASS THE BOOK TO JESTER 2 ➡

Jokes

JESTER 2

What do you call it when a shoe is busy?

Tied up!

/1

What is an anvil's favorite kind of music?

Heavy Metal.

/1

Why was the janitor late for school?

He over swept!

/1

What movie is the best to watch on April 1st?

/1

PRANK-enstein!

JOKES TOTAL: /4

Silly Scenarios

(Act it out!)

You are a caveman who just heard music for the first time. What do your cave man dance moves look like?

/2

You're rowing down the river when you see something scary ahead! Look as frightened as possible and try to paddle your canoe backward, **QUICKLY!**

/2

SILLY SCENARIOS TOTAL: _____ /4

TIME TO SCORE YOUR POINTS! →

JESTER 1

/8

ROUND TOTAL

JESTER 2

/8

ROUND TOTAL

ROUND
CHAMPION

ROUND 3

Jokes

What is it called when all the checker pieces don't want to play?

_____ /1

A BORED game.

What did the cannibal say to the zombie in the graveyard?

_____ /1

"You gonna eat that?"

Why do you throw away a broken watch?

_____ /1

It's a waste of time!

Why are robots so brave?

They have nerves of steel.

_____ /1

JOKES TOTAL: _____ /4

Silly Scenarios

(Act it out!)

You're a clumsy skeleton made entirely of funny bones, and every time you bump into something you can't stop laughing!

/2

Hop like a frog with the jumping hiccups! Each time you hiccup, you "ribbit", and each time you "ribbit", you JUMP!

/2

SILLY SCENARIOS TOTAL: _____ /4

 NOW, PASS THE BOOK TO JESTER 2 ➡

Jokes

What kind of vehicle does a baby paramedic drive?

A Wahhh-mbulance!

_/1

How did the girl feel after getting rained on?

Under the weather.

_/1

Why did the happy clock soar through the sky?

Because time flies when it's having fun!

_/1

Why do libraries make such good vacation spots?

_/1

They're always easy to BOOK!

JOKES TOTAL: _/4

JESTER 2 CONTINUE TO THE NEXT PAGE →

Silly Scenarios

(Act it out!)

Pretend your car runs off the road and is balancing on the edge of a giant cliff. Every move makes the car start to tip over! Try to get out before it goes down!

/2

Every time you talk, **YOU CAN ONLY SCREAM!** Have a conversation with your friend in the library, as you *silently* scream everything!

/2

SILLY SCENARIOS TOTAL: _____ /4

TIME TO SCORE YOUR POINTS! ➡️

JESTER 1

/8

ROUND TOTAL

JESTER 2

/8

ROUND TOTAL

ROUND CHAMPION

ROUND
4

Jokes

What kind of stories do wigs like to tell?

Hairy Tales.

_____ /1

Where can a dog go to sell his collar?

The PAW-n Shop.

_____ /1

Why did 'B' run into a wall?

He couldn't 'C'.

_____ /1

Did you hear about the man who makes shoes for elephants? No? Well let me tell you, it's no small feet.

_____ /1

JOKES TOTAL: _____ /4

Silly Scenarios

(Act it out!)

Pretend you just stepped in something nasty. Try to take your dirty shoe off without getting anything on the carpet or on yourself. GROSS!

/2

Act like a blindfolded monkey trying to hit a piñata. Make sure you walk and talk like a monkey!

/2

SILLY SCENARIOS TOTAL: _____ /4

 NOW, PASS THE BOOK TO JESTER 2 ➡

31

Jokes

JESTER 2

What's the name of the royal DJ with the circular speakers?

Sir Round Sound!

/1

How do you become a railroad conductor?

Lots of TRAIN-ing.

/1

Why couldn't the french fry find a job?

He was being a lazy couch potato!

/1

What is the Star Wars Jedi's favorite candy?

/1

A Life-Saver.

JOKES TOTAL: /4

Silly Scenarios

(Act it out!)

Pretend you have an extra heavy tongue. Try to tell your friends something, but every time your mouth opens to talk, your tongue just falls out!

_____ /2

You're a weatherman in the middle of an important update, but suddenly you fall on your knees, laughing hysterically because you feel like you're being tickled all over!

_____ /2

SILLY SCENARIOS TOTAL: _____ /4

TIME TO SCORE YOUR POINTS! ➜

JESTER 1

/8
——————
ROUND TOTAL

JESTER 2

/8
——————
ROUND TOTAL

——————
ROUND
CHAMPION

ROUND
5

Jokes

Where do you go to see the sneak preview of upcoming movies?

To the TRAILER Park!

/1

The monkey in the Zoo turned out to just be a kid in a costume. Now that's what I call a CHIMP-oster!

/1

Why did the man dig a hole to sleep in?

To get some deep sleep!

/1

How did the biker help the environment?

/1

By re-CYCLING!

JOKES TOTAL: _____ /4

Silly Scenarios

(Act it out!)

Pretend that with every step you take, you get electrocuted! Try to make it from one side of the room to the other!

_____ /2

You're a squirrel digging for nuts and you can't seem to find your favorite nut that you've been thinking about all winter! Make confusing, chittering sounds as you search.

_____ /2

SILLY SCENARIOS TOTAL: _____ /4

NOW, PASS THE BOOK TO JESTER 2 ➡

Jokes

How do you fix a broken cake?
Glue it together and call it a PASTE-ry!

/1

What's an avocado's favorite arcade game?
Whack-a-mole-y!

/1

What did the fisherman say to the fish, when he threw it back into the water?
"You're off the hook!"

/1

What is the only toy a tired cat will play with?

/1

A ball of YAWN.

JOKES TOTAL: ___ /4

Silly Scenarios

(Act it out!)

Dogs are a man's best friend. Pretend you're a dog that's laying on its back and **REALLY** wants a belly rub. Don't stop trying until your friend gives you one!

/2

You are a crab scuttling sideways on the beach. Snap your pinchers at people and sway your head side to side, so everyone knows how dangerous you are!

/2

SILLY SCENARIOS TOTAL: _____ /4

TIME TO SCORE YOUR POINTS! ➡

JESTER 1

/8

ROUND TOTAL

JESTER 2

/8

ROUND TOTAL

ROUND
CHAMPION

ROUND
6

Jokes

What's a trampoline's favorite season?

Spring! ___/1

What do martial artists use to make cookies?

Tae-Kwon-DOUGH! ___/1

Which animal in the Arctic is the best writer?

A PEN-guin. ___/1

Where do you put awards for similarity?

The Hall of Same. ___/1

JOKES TOTAL: ___/4

JESTER 1 CONTINUE TO THE NEXT PAGE ➞

Silly Scenarios

(Act it out!)

It's your first day as a dog-walker! Pretend you're trying to walk 10 different dogs, but they all want to go in different directions AND their leashes keep getting tangled up!

/2

You are crossing a river using only tiny stepping stones. It's very hard to balance on them, so do your best not to fall over!

/2

SILLY SCENARIOS TOTAL: _____ /4

NOW, PASS THE BOOK TO JESTER 2 ➡

Jokes

What did one cat say to the other cat?

"Have a mice day!"   /1

Why did the firefly keep raising its hand in class?

It had to GLOW to the bathroom!   /1

Why is it hard to hang out with a chicken?

They have foul breath!   /1

What coat do dogs love most?

PARK-a.   /1

JOKES TOTAL: _____ /4

JESTER 2 CONTINUE TO THE NEXT PAGE →

Silly Scenarios

(Act it out!)

You are a funky, dancing worm! Show off your moves and remember, no using arms!

_____ /2

You're a giant wild monkey who just drank a whole bottle of hot sauce that he thought was chocolate milk... UH-OH!

_____ /2

SILLY SCENARIOS TOTAL: _____ /4

TIME TO SCORE YOUR POINTS! ➡

JESTER 1

 /8

ROUND TOTAL

JESTER 2

 /8

ROUND TOTAL

ROUND
CHAMPION

ROUND
7

Jokes

Do you know why cats never finish watching movies?

I heard they always PAWS it half-way through.   /1

I saw a bully step all over someone's new shoes today. It was sole-crushing to watch.   /1

Which day of the week is McDonald's favorite?

FRY-day!   /1

Why did the lime break up with the lemon?

Not sure, but she's still sour about it.   /1

JOKES TOTAL: _____ /4

Silly Scenarios

(Act it out!)

You are a baby learning to crawl, but you keep bumping into things and it's making you cry every time. WAHHH!

/2

You're in Antarctica and you are **FREEZING!** Your teeth chatter and you are shivering. Rub your arms and blow on your hands to try and stay warm. As you move around, you notice that your movements are getting stiffer and stiffer, until you finally end up frozen in a silly position!

/2

SILLY SCENARIOS TOTAL: _____ /4

NOW, PASS THE BOOK TO JESTER 2 ➡

Jokes

Who is Barbie's favorite football team?

The Miami DOLL-phins!

/1

What do bees like to do in their free time?

Work on jigsaw BUZZ-les!

/1

Why did the oreo go to college?

He wanted to be a smart cookie.

/1

Why are bodybuilders so impatient?

They've been WEIGHTing their whole lives!

/1

JOKES TOTAL: _____ /4

JESTER 2 CONTINUE TO THE NEXT PAGE ➜

Silly Scenarios

(Act it out!)

You are a chimp who just found ice cream...
and also just discovered a **BRAIN FREEZE!**

_____ **/2**

Backward Planet - You are an alien from a
world where everything is done in reverse.
Show how you would read a book or eat a
meal in reverse!

_____ **/2**

SILLY SCENARIOS TOTAL: _____ **/4**

TIME TO SCORE YOUR POINTS! ➡

JESTER 1

/8

ROUND TOTAL

JESTER 2

/8

ROUND TOTAL

ROUND
CHAMPION

ROUND

8

Jokes

What does cereal like to do for fun?

They love to go **BOWL**-ing!   /1

Who is ramen's favorite hero?

SOUP-er Man.   /1

Why was the lightbulb so curious?

He wanted to know **WATTS** up!   /1

What do you call a bird of prey that becomes a pirate?

Captain Hawk.   /1

JOKES TOTAL: _____ /4

Silly Scenarios

(Act it out!) JESTER 1

The year is 3030 and you're flying a plane. Hungry? There's a fly-thru lane at Mcdonald's! Pretend to fly through, grab your order, and continue on your journey!

_____ /2

You are a sleepy bear just waking up from hibernation, but you wake up to strange sounds. You crawl out of your cave only to discover you're now in Jurassic Park! Hurry, RUN!

_____ /2

SILLY SCENARIOS TOTAL: _____ /4

NOW, PASS THE BOOK TO JESTER 2 ➡

Jokes

What do you call a positive Manta?

A RAY of sunshine.

/1

What kind of horse wears flippers instead of horseshoes?

A Sea Horse!

/1

What bird doesn't like cars?

A Roadrunner, duh.

/1

Why is it hard to reason with a kangaroo?

They always JUMP to conclusions!

/1

JOKES TOTAL: _____ /4

JESTER 2 CONTINUE TO THE NEXT PAGE →

Silly Scenarios

(Act it out!)

You're a duck waddling around. Give your best impression of a laughing duck while waddling!

_____ /2

Congratulations! Your parents got you a puppy, but oh no, it has fleas... and now so do you! You're so, **SO ITCHY!**

_____ /2

SILLY SCENARIOS TOTAL: _____ /4

TIME TO SCORE YOUR POINTS! ➔

57

 **JESTER 1**  **/8**

ROUND TOTAL

 **JESTER 2**  **/8**

ROUND TOTAL

ROUND CHAMPION

ROUND

9

Jokes

What's the difference between dough and the sun?

One rises in the yeast, the other sets in the west!

/1

The nickels and dimes got tired of doing the same thing every day. They needed some CHANGE.

/1

Where do winter shoes spend their summers?

Boot Camp.

/1

What did the broccoli get his wife for Valentine's Day?

/1

A bouquet of cauliflowers.

JOKES TOTAL: /4

JESTER 1 CONTINUE TO THE NEXT PAGE →

Silly Scenarios

(Act it out!)

You're playing tag with a friend, running through the house as fast as possible. Then BOOM! - You run into a glass door! Pretend to fall back, then move your head like you're really dizzy!

_____ /2

You've been asked to play "Happy Birthday" for your teacher on the piano, but turns out the piano only makes burping noises!

_____ /2

SILLY SCENARIOS TOTAL: _____ /4

NOW, PASS THE BOOK TO JESTER 2 ➡

Jokes

JESTER 2

How did the family stay dry during the rainstorm?

It just barely MIST them.   /1

What is a rock's favorite band?

The Rolling Stones!   /1

What do you call it when rabbits misbehave?

A bad HARE day!   /1

Why did the ABC's go to the casino?

They wanted to make an alpha-BET!   /1

JOKES TOTAL: _____ /4

Silly Scenarios

(Act it out!)

Pretend you're a giant walking through New York City, trying not to step on anyone!

/2

You're a noble knight that is in the middle of slaying a ticklish, fire-breathing dragon!

/2

SILLY SCENARIOS TOTAL: _____ /4

TIME TO SCORE YOUR POINTS! ➡️ 63

 JESTER 1

/8

ROUND TOTAL

 JESTER 2

/8

ROUND TOTAL

ROUND
CHAMPION

ROUND

10

Jokes

Where is the most positive place to put your garbage?

A trash CAN!

_____ /1

What did the deck of cards say when it got 100% on it's test?

"Aced it!"

_____ /1

The oyster only cares about himself, he's so shellfish.

_____ /1

Why was the band trying to gain more weight?

To be better at heavy metal!

_____ /1

JOKES TOTAL: _____ /4

Silly Scenarios

(Act it out!)

Your mom has asked you to mop the floor, but to make it more fun you've decided to wear rollerskates! Demonstrate how it's done while groovin' to the music!

_____ /2

Pretend to be a wolf that loves to play hockey. Take a shot at the goal with your hockey stick and let out a big, roaring howl of victory!

_____ /2

SILLY SCENARIOS TOTAL: _____ /4

NOW, PASS THE BOOK TO JESTER 2 ➡

Jokes

What style of dance is something you find on a playground?

/1

Swing!

Why did the man like operating a jackhammer?

/1

It was groundbreaking work!

Why can't you trust the fastest animal in the world?

/1

Because it's a CHEAT-ah!

What dog lives underground?

/1

A Prairie Dog!

JOKES TOTAL: _____ /4

Silly Scenarios

(Act it out!)

You are a zombie in a music video.
Demonstrate how zombies dance and jam out!

_____ /2

Welcome to old age. Walk like an old man
then bust out into an old man boogie!

_____ /2

SILLY SCENARIOS TOTAL: _____ /4

TIME TO SCORE YOUR POINTS! →

 **JESTER 1**

 **/8**

ROUND TOTAL

 **JESTER 2**

 **/8**

ROUND TOTAL

ROUND CHAMPION

ADD UP ALL YOUR POINTS FROM EACH ROUND.
THE PLAYER WITH THE MOST POINTS IS CROWNED
THE ULTIMATE LAUGH MASTER!

IN THE EVENT OF A TIE, CONTINUE TO THE ROUND
11 FOR THE TIE-BREAKER ROUND!

JESTER 1 _____
GRAND TOTAL

JESTER 2 _____
GRAND TOTAL

_____
**THE ULTIMATE
DON'T LAUGH CHALLENGE MASTER**

ROUND

11

TIE-BREAKER

(WINNER TAKES ALL!)

Jokes

What do aliens use to fix everything?

Ab-DUCT tape!

/1

Why did the baker get a second job?

He needed the extra dough.

/1

Why is the sun losing followers?

Too many people use sun-BLOCK!

/1

What do cowboys put on their sandwiches?

HORSE-radish.

/1

JOKES TOTAL: _____ /4

Silly Scenarios

(Act it out!)

Row, row, row your boat across a lake full of gravy, so thick that it takes all your strength to move the oars. Do whatever it takes to get to the other side, even if that means eating it!

_____ /2

You're a busy bumble bee buzzing from flower to flower, but you're allergic to pollen and can't stop sneezing!

_____ /2

SILLY SCENARIOS TOTAL: _____ /4

 NOW, PASS THE BOOK TO JESTER 2 ➡

Jokes

Why did the man clean his glasses?
He didn't want to give anyone dirty looks.   /1

What did the Sharpie study in college?
MARK-it-ing!   /1

What vegetable always wanted to be a salesman?
SELL-ery!   /1

What do you call a fish that is also a carpenter?
A Hammerhead!   /1

JOKES TOTAL: /4

Silly Scenarios

(Act it out!)

Whenever you hug someone, your arms get stuck and **YOU CAN'T LET GO!** Now hug your friend! (Be nice and don't hold them for too long!)

_____ /2

Your friend pranked you! Now, you're glued to a rolly-chair, and you have to roll everywhere you go!

_____ /2

SILLY SCENARIOS TOTAL: _____ /4

TIME TO SCORE YOUR POINTS! ➡

ADD UP ALL YOUR POINTS FROM THE PREVIOUS ROUND. THE JESTER WITH THE MOST POINTS IS CROWNED THE ULTIMATE DON'T LAUGH CHALLENGE MASTER!

JESTER 1

/8

_____

GRAND TOTAL

JESTER 2

/8

_____

GRAND TOTAL

_____

THE ULTIMATE
DON'T LAUGH CHALLENGE MASTER

Check out our

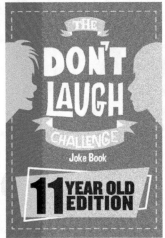

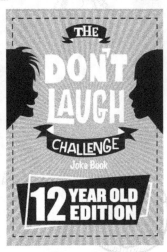

Visit us at
www.DontLaughChallenge.com
to check out our newest books!

other joke books!

If you have enjoyed our book, we would love for you to review us on Amazon!